P9-BIP-878

FAMILY MEALS

Julia Roles

🦁 GOLDEN PRESS / NEW YORK

Western Publishing Company, Inc.
Racine, Wisconsin

CONTENTS

This edition prepared under the supervision of
Joanna Morris

This edition published 1984 by Golden Press
Library of Congress Catalog Card Number: 84-80338
ISBN 0-307-09965-2
Golden® and Golden Press® are registered trademarks
of Western Publishing Company, Inc.

First published in 1980 in the U.K. by Cathay Books,
59 Grosvenor Street, London W1

© 1984, 1983, 1982, 1980, 1979 Cathay Books

Printed in Hong Kong

INTRODUCTION

All too frequently the term "family meals" is associated with boring, uninteresting foods. That's not the way it has to be—or ought to be. It's true that today's cooks have far less time to spend in the kitchen. But it's equally true that there are many quick-to-fix, inexpensive dishes which are a little out of the ordinary, and which can certainly brighten up the dinner table. All it takes is a little thought to make "routine" foods special.

The following pages offer a tempting selection of just such recipes. You'll find sure-fire favorites, such as Easy Swiss Steak and Southern Fried Chicken, as well as more adventurous recipes for Pork in Applejack and Salmon Steaks in Vermouth. Included, too, are soups and light supper dishes, vegetables, salads and mouth-watering desserts. With recipes like these, you'll discover that family meals are delicious meals.

NOTES:

Always preheat the oven to the specified temperature.

Margarine can be substituted for butter in all recipes.

If substituting dried herbs for fresh, use a third of the amount;
if substituting fresh for dried,
use 3 times the amount.

SOUPS & LIGHT SUPPERS

Carrot and Orange Soup

2 tablespoons butter
1 tablespoon oil
1 lb carrots, sliced
2 medium onions, chopped
3 tablespoons flour
4 cups chicken stock or broth
Grated rind and juice of ½ orange
Juice of ½ lemon
Salt and pepper

In a large saucepan, melt the butter in the oil over moderate heat. Add the carrots and onions; sauté until tender. Sprinkle flour over the vegetables and sauté, stirring, for about 1 minute. Remove from heat and stir in stock.

Return to the heat and bring to a boil, stirring. Stir in the orange rind, orange juice, lemon juice and salt and pepper to taste. Reduce the heat to low, cover and simmer for about 30 minutes.

Transfer the mixture to a blender and puree. Heat through just before serving.

4 to 6 servings

Quick Cold Cucumber Soup

1 large cucumber,
  peeled, seeded and
  coarsely grated
2 cups plain yogurt
½ cup sour cream
Salt and pepper
1 to 2 tablespoons
  finely chopped
  mint

In a medium mixing bowl, combine the cucumber, yogurt, sour cream and salt and pepper to taste. Chill for at least 2 hours, until just before serving.

Stir in the chopped mint. Pour into chilled bowls and garnish with mint sprigs if desired.

4 servings

Gazpacho

1 lb tomatoes, peeled and chopped
1 medium onion, chopped
1 small green pepper, seeded and chopped
1 clove garlic, crushed
1 tablespoon white wine vinegar
2 tablespoons olive oil
2 tablespoons lemon juice
1 slice white bread, crusts removed
1¼ cups chicken stock or broth
Salt and pepper
Diced cucumber
Croutons

Combine all ingredients except the cucumber and croutons in a food processor or blender and process until very smooth. Cover and chill for at least 2 hours.

Serve the diced cucumber and croutons in separate dishes and pass at the table.

4 servings

Split Pea and Ham Soup

1 cup (8 oz) split
  peas, rinsed and
  sorted
1 small smoked ham
  hock
6 cups water
4 tablespoons butter
1 medium onion,
  chopped
2 potatoes, peeled
  and cubed
2 stalks celery,
  chopped
Salt and pepper

In a large saucepan, combine peas, ham hock and water, and bring to a boil over high heat. Cover, reduce heat and simmer for about 3 hours.

Meanwhile, melt the butter in a medium skillet. Add the onion, potatoes and celery and sauté until all vegetables are tender.

When the ham hock is cool enough to handle, remove the meat, discarding fat and bone; dice and set aside.

Remove the saucepan from the heat; let cool slightly. Transfer mixture to a food processor, blender or food mill and puree. Return the puree to the saucepan. Add diced ham, salt and pepper to taste and heat through.
6 to 8 servings

French Vegetable Soup

4 slices bacon, diced
2 medium onions,
  chopped
2 large leeks,
  chopped
1 parsnip, chopped
2 carrots, chopped
1 medium potato,
  chopped
4 cups beef stock or
  broth
1 can (8 oz) whole
  tomatoes
2 bay leaves
¼ teaspoon dried
  thyme
1 tablespoon
  chopped parsley
Salt and pepper

In a large saucepan, sauté the bacon until brown. Add the onions, leeks, parsnip, carrots and potato and sauté until softened. Stir in the stock, tomatoes and their juice, bay leaves, thyme, parsley, salt and pepper. Bring to a boil over high heat. Cover, reduce heat and simmer for 30 to 45 minutes or until the vegetables are tender. Remove from heat and let cool slightly.

Remove bay leaves. Transfer mixture to a food processor, blender or food mill and process until smooth. Return to the pan and heat through before serving.

4 to 6 servings

Leek and Potato Soup

4 tablespoons butter
1 tablespoon oil
6 leeks, sliced
4 medium potatoes, sliced
5 cups chicken stock or broth
Salt and pepper
Pinch of grated nutmeg
¾ cup half-and-half

In a large saucepan, melt the butter in the oil. Add leeks and sauté until softened, about 10 minutes. Add potatoes, stock, salt, pepper and nutmeg. Cover and simmer over low heat for about 30 minutes, or until the vegetables are tender. Remove from heat; let cool slightly.

Transfer to a food processor, blender or food mill and process until smooth. Stir in the half-and-half.

If the soup is to be served cold, chill for at least 2 hours, until just before serving. Or, if you prefer, return the soup to saucepan, heat through, without allowing to boil, and serve hot. Garnish with chopped chives.

6 servings

French Onion Soup

4 tablespoons butter
4 large onions, sliced
1½ tablespoons flour
4 cups beef stock or broth
Salt and pepper
4 to 6 slices French bread
½ cup grated sharp Cheddar cheese

In a large saucepan, melt the butter. Stir in the onions and sauté until softened. Sprinkle in the flour and continue to sauté, stirring, until lightly browned.

Remove from the heat and gradually add stock. Bring to a boil, stirring. Add salt and pepper to taste, reduce heat and simmer for 30 minutes.

Pour into individual flameproof bowls. Float a slice of French bread in each bowl and sprinkle generously with cheese. Place bowls on a baking sheet and broil until the tops are golden and bubbling.

4 to 6 servings

Cream of Lettuce Soup

6 tablespoons butter
1 medium head lettuce, shredded
1 medium onion, finely chopped
2½ cups chicken stock or broth
Salt and pepper
1 teaspoon sugar
1¼ cups milk
1 onion stuck with 4 cloves
4 peppercorns
Pinch of grated nutmeg
4 tablespoons flour

Melt 4 tablespoons of the butter in a large saucepan. Add the lettuce and chopped onion and sauté over low heat for 10 minutes, stirring occasionally. Stir in the stock, salt, pepper and sugar. Cover and simmer for 30 minutes.

In a separate saucepan, combine the milk, onion, peppercorns and nutmeg. Bring to a boil. Cover, remove from heat and let stand 15 minutes.

Melt the remaining 2 tablespoons of butter in a medium saucepan. Stir in the flour and cook, stirring, for about 1 minute. Remove from the heat.

Meanwhile, strain the warm milk, discarding the onion and peppercorns. Gradually stir the milk into the butter and flour mixture. Bring to a boil, stirring constantly. Add the milk mixture to the lettuce, mixing well, and simmer for 10 minutes; cool slightly.

Transfer to a blender and process until smooth. Heat before serving. Or, if serving cold, chill at least 2 hours. Garnish with croutons if desired.

4 to 6 servings

Individual Pita Pizzas

4 tablespoons
tomato sauce
4 pita breads
1 lb ripe tomatoes,
thinly sliced
4 oz mushrooms,
thinly sliced
½ to 1 teaspoon
garlic salt
½ to 1 teaspoon
dried marjoram
½ to 1 teaspoon
dried basil
Salt and pepper
1 cup grated Cheddar
cheese

Spread a thin layer of tomato sauce over the top of each pita bread. Arrange tomato slices and mushrooms on top; sprinkle with garlic salt, herbs, salt, pepper and grated cheese.

Place the pitas on a greased baking sheet and bake in a 400° oven for 15 minutes, or until the cheese is melted and golden and the pitas are heated through.

4 servings

Pizza alla Napolitana

1 package (16 oz)
   frozen pizza dough
   or white bread
   dough
2 tablespoons oil
1 medium onion,
   chopped
3/4 lb tomatoes,
   chopped
1 can (8 oz) tomato
   sauce
1 teaspoon sugar
Salt and pepper
1 clove garlic,
   crushed
1 bay leaf
1 teaspoon dried
   oregano or
   marjoram
4 oz mozzarella
   cheese, sliced
1 can (2 oz) anchovy
   fillets, drained
20 pitted ripe olives

Thaw the dough according to package directions and roll or pat out to a 9- or 10-inch circle. Place on a greased baking sheet and chill until ready to use.

In a large skillet, heat the oil. Add the onion and sauté until softened. Stir in the tomatoes, tomato sauce, sugar, salt, pepper, garlic, bay leaf and oregano. Simmer over low heat for 10 to 15 minutes, or until the sauce thickens. Remove from heat; let cool and remove bay leaf.

Spread the sauce over the chilled dough, leaving a 3/4-inch edge all around. Lay the cheese slices on top. Arrange the anchovies in a lattice pattern over cheese and place an olive in each lattice square. Let rise in a warm place for 15 minutes.

Bake in a 425° oven for 20 to 25 minutes. Serve hot.

Makes one 10-inch pizza

Cheddar and Bacon Quiche

1½ cups all-purpose flour
½ teaspoon salt
3 tablespoons chilled butter
3 tablespoons chilled shortening
2 to 3 tablespoons ice water
6 slices bacon, diced
1 small onion, thinly sliced
FILLING:
½ cup grated Cheddar cheese
2 eggs, beaten
1 tablespoon chopped parsley (optional)
⅔ cup milk
Salt and pepper

Combine the flour and salt in a bowl. Cut the butter and shortening into small pieces and work into the flour until mixture resembles coarse crumbs. Add 1 tablespoon of water at a time, continuing to mix. Form into a ball. Cover and chill for 30 minutes.

Meanwhile, sauté the bacon and the onion. Drain and set aside. Combine the filling ingredients.

Roll out the dough into a circle about 10 inches in diameter. Place in an 8-inch quiche pan and prick with a fork. Line with foil and fill with dried beans. Chill briefly.

Bake in a 400° oven for 10 minutes. Remove foil and beans. Spread the onion and bacon over the pie shell. Pour in the filling. Return to the oven and bake for 25 to 30 minutes, until set.
4 to 6 servings

Scalloped Potatoes and Ham

½ teaspoon garlic
   salt
1½ lb potatoes,
   thinly sliced
Salt and pepper
Grated nutmeg
2 cups chopped
   cooked ham
2 cups grated
   Cheddar cheese
1¼ cups milk

Butter a 2-quart casserole and sprinkle
with garlic salt. Arrange a third of the
potatoes in the bottom of the casserole, sprinkle with salt, pepper and
nutmeg. Sprinkle with a third of the
ham and a third of the grated cheese.
Repeat layering twice. Pour the milk
over the top.
   Bake in a 350° oven for about 1 hour,
or until the potatoes are tender when
pierced with a fork.
6 servings

17

Cheddar and Cider Fondue

½ small onion
1¼ cups hard dry cider or dry white wine
1 teaspoon lemon juice
1 lb Cheddar cheese, grated
1 tablespoon cornstarch
2 tablespoons dry sherry
Pinch of dry mustard
1 teaspoon Worcestershire sauce
Pepper
1 large loaf French bread, cut into bite-size cubes

Rub the side and bottom of a heavy medium saucepan or fondue pot with the cut surface of the onion. Add the cider and lemon juice and simmer over moderate heat until bubbling. Gradually add the cheese and simmer, stirring constantly, until it melts completely; do not boil.

In a small bowl, combine the cornstarch, sherry, mustard, Worcestershire sauce and pepper. Stir into melted cheese mixture and simmer over low heat, stirring, for 2 or 3 minutes, or until the fondue is thick and creamy.

Serve hot, surrounded by the bread cubes to be dipped into the fondue.

6 servings

Swiss Cheese Fondue

1 clove garlic, cut in half lengthwise
⅔ cup dry white wine
1 teaspoon lemon juice
12 oz Swiss cheese, grated
1 teaspoon cornstarch
2 tablespoons kirsch or brandy
Pepper
Pinch of grated nutmeg
1 large loaf French bread, cut into bite-size cubes

Rub the side and bottom of a heavy medium saucepan or fondue pot with the cut surface of the garlic. Add the wine and lemon juice and simmer over moderate heat until bubbling. Gradually add the cheese and simmer, stirring constantly, until it melts completely; do not boil.

In a small bowl, blend the cornstarch and kirsch. Stir it into the melted cheese mixture and simmer over low heat, stirring, for 2 or 3 minutes, or until the fondue is thick and creamy. Add pepper and nutmeg to taste.

Serve hot, surrounded by the bread cubes to be dipped into the fondue.

4 to 6 servings

Eggs in Curry Sauce

8 eggs
2 tablespoons oil
2 onions, coarsely
   chopped
2 cloves garlic,
   crushed
1 tablespoon finely
   chopped fresh
   gingerroot or
   ½ teaspoon
   ground ginger
½ teaspoon ground
   cinnamon
1 teaspoon paprika
1 teaspoon salt
1 tablespoon mild
   curry powder
2 tablespoons flaked
   coconut
6 tablespoons
   pineapple juice
1¼ cups chicken
   stock or broth
1¼ cups plain yogurt

Cover the eggs with water in a saucepan. Bring to a boil over moderate heat and boil gently for 5 minutes. Meanwhile, heat the oil in a large skillet. Add the onions, garlic and gingerroot and sauté for 3 minutes. Add the cinnamon, paprika, salt and curry powder. Reduce heat and cook gently about 10 minutes, stirring occasionally.

Shell the eggs. Stir the coconut, pineapple juice, stock and yogurt into the spice mixture. Add the eggs and simmer for 20 minutes.

Serve hot with cooked rice. Curry is traditionally accompanied by a variety of side dishes, such as chopped onion and tomato, toasted coconut, sliced cucumber in yogurt, sliced bananas and chutney.

4 servings

Classic Cheese Soufflé

4 tablespoons butter
3 tablespoons flour
1¼ cups milk
4 eggs, separated
¾ cup grated
    Gruyère or Swiss
    cheese
1 tablespoon grated
    Parmesan cheese
¼ teaspoon prepared
    mustard
Salt and pepper

Melt the butter in a large saucepan. Stir in the flour and cook for about 1 minute. Remove from the heat and gradually blend in the milk. Return the saucepan to moderate heat and simmer, stirring, until thickened. Remove from the heat and blend in the yolks, cheeses, mustard, salt and pepper.

Whisk the egg whites until stiff but not dry. Fold a quarter of the whites into the cheese mixture. Then gently fold in remaining whites.

Turn the mixture into a well-greased 1½-quart soufflé dish. Bake in a 375° oven for 35 to 40 minutes, or until well risen. Serve immediately.

4 servings

Variations: Use only ¼ cup grated cheese. Add ¼ cup of any of the following to the basic sauce: chopped chicken, ham or mushrooms; peeled small shrimp; flaked white fish.

MEAT & POULTRY

Marinated Beef Kabobs

½ cup Italian salad
   dressing
1 lb beef, cut into
   1½-inch cubes
16 medium
   mushrooms
16 cherry tomatoes
16 pearl onions
2 large green
   peppers, cut into
   1½-inch squares

Pour the dressing over the meat in a medium mixing bowl and stir to coat. Cover, refrigerate and allow to marinate several hours or overnight.

Thread 8 metal skewers, alternating meat, mushroom, tomato, onion and pepper. Reserve marinade.

Place the skewers on a rack in the broiler, 3 to 4 inches from the heat. Broil for 6 to 8 minutes, turning frequently and brushing with marinade. Serve on a bed of rice.

4 servings

Easy Swiss Steak

¼ cup flour
Salt and pepper
1¼ lb round steak,
    cut into 4 portions
3 tablespoons oil
2 large onions,
    chopped
1 package (¾ oz) beef
    gravy mix
1 tablespoon
    prepared brown
    mustard

Season the flour with salt and pepper and dredge the meat.

In a large skillet, heat the oil; add the meat and brown quickly on both sides over moderately high heat. Reduce heat, add the onions and cook until softened. Transfer the meat and onions to a 1-quart casserole.

Prepare the gravy according to the package directions. Stir in the mustard. Pour the gravy over the meat. Cover and cook in a 350° oven for 1½ to 2 hours, or until the meat is tender. Garnish with parsley.

4 servings

Spaghetti Bolognese

4 tablespoons butter
2 tablespoons oil
2 medium onions,
 chopped
1 lb lean ground beef
½ lb mushrooms,
 chopped
1 can (16 oz) whole
 tomatoes
2 cloves garlic,
 crushed
½ teaspoon dried
 oregano
¼ cup tomato paste
⅔ cup beef stock,
 broth or red wine
Salt and pepper
¾ lb spaghetti
Grated nutmeg
Grated Parmesan
 cheese

In a large saucepan, heat 2 tablespoons of the butter in the oil over moderate heat. Add the onions and sauté until softened. Add the meat and cook until evenly browned, stirring to break up meat. Drain off excess fat. Add the mushrooms, tomatoes and their juice, garlic, oregano, tomato paste and stock. Season with salt and pepper. Cover and simmer over low heat for 1 hour, adding more liquid if necessary.

Fifteen minutes before serving, cook the spaghetti in boiling salted water according to package directions. Drain thoroughly. Turn into a serving dish and toss with the remaining 2 tablespoons butter. Season to taste with nutmeg.

Top with sauce and sprinkle with Parmesan cheese.

4 servings

Irish Stew

2 lb stewing lamb
 (boned shoulder or
 neck), cut into
 1½-inch cubes
Salt and pepper
3 large onions, sliced
2 lb potatoes, sliced
2 tablespoons
 Worcestershire
 sauce

Trim the lamb of any excess fat and gristle. Arrange in the bottom of a large, heavy flameproof casserole or Dutch oven. Sprinkle with salt and pepper. Cover with a layer of onions and then potatoes. Continue to alternate layers of onions and potatoes until all have been used. Sprinkle with Worcestershire sauce.

Add enough water to barely cover the top layer of potatoes. Bring to a boil on the top of the stove. Cover and cook in a 325° oven for 2½ hours.

4 to 6 servings

Beef and Pepper Bake

3 tablespoons flour
Salt and pepper
2 lb stewing beef, cut
   into 1-inch cubes
3 tablespoons oil
3 medium onions,
   chopped
1 large green pepper,
   seeded and
   chopped
2½ cups beef stock
   or broth or a
   mixture of stock
   and red wine
Bouquet garni or
   ½ teaspoon dried
   thyme and 2 bay
   leaves
½ lb mushrooms,
   sliced

Season the flour with salt and pepper and use to coat the meat. Reserve any remaining flour. Heat the oil in a deep flameproof casserole or Dutch oven and brown the beef in batches over moderately high heat. Transfer the browned beef to a large bowl.

Add the onions and green pepper to the casserole and sauté until softened. Return the beef to the casserole, sprinkle in any remaining flour and cook, stirring, for 1 minute.

Gradually stir in the stock and bring to a boil over moderately high heat, stirring constantly. Add the bouquet garni. Cover and bake in a 325° oven for 2 hours.

Add the mushrooms, adjust the seasonings, if necessary, and bake for 30 minutes longer.

Remove the bouquet garni; serve with boiled new potatoes and a tossed green salad.

4 to 6 servings

Braised Oxtails

4 lb oxtails, cut into
2-inch lengths
4 tablespoons beef
drippings or oil
4 medium onions,
chopped
4 carrots, sliced
3 stalks celery,
chopped
1 small turnip, finely
chopped
2 tablespoons flour
3 cups beef stock or
broth
Salt and pepper
Grated nutmeg
Bouquet garni or
½ teaspoon dried
thyme and 2 bay
leaves

Trim the oxtails of any excess fat. Heat the beef drippings in a deep flameproof casserole or Dutch oven. Add the oxtails and brown quickly on all sides over a high heat. Transfer to a large bowl.

Add the onions, carrots, celery and turnip to the casserole and sauté until softened. Sprinkle in the flour and cook, stirring, until the mixture begins to brown. Gradually add the stock and bring to a boil, stirring constantly.

Return the oxtails to the casserole, season with salt, pepper and nutmeg and add the bouquet garni. Bake in a 300° oven for 4 hours, adding more stock or water if necessary.

Remove from the oven; let cool and refrigerate overnight. To serve, skim off the fat that has accumulated on the surface, then simmer over moderately low heat for 30 minutes. Remove the bouquet garni.

6 servings

Tongue with Sherry Sauce

1 smoked beef
  tongue (3½ lb)
1 whole onion
2 bay leaves
3 tablespoons butter
4 tablespoons flour
⅔ cup sweet sherry
2 tablespoons
  currant jelly

Place the tongue in a large heavy pot. Cover with cold water and bring to a boil; boil for 5 minutes. Drain, discarding the water. Return the tongue to the pot and add cold water to cover. Add the onion and bay leaves. Bring to a boil. Reduce heat and simmer for 2½ to 3 hours, skimming the surface frequently.

About 15 or 20 minutes before the tongue is finished cooking, spoon out ⅔ cup of its cooking liquid for the sauce. Melt the butter in a small saucepan and stir in the flour. Gradually stir in the sherry and cooking liquid and bring to a boil. Reduce heat and simmer for 5 minutes.

Meanwhile, drain the tongue and plunge into cold water. Peel off the skin and remove any bones. Slice tongue thickly and arrange on a warmed serving platter.

Stir the jelly into the sauce and pour over tongue. Garnish with watercress sprigs if desired.

6 servings.

Savory Pot Roast

3 tablespoons olive oil
1 beef round rump roast (3 to 3½ lb)
Salt and pepper
2 cloves garlic, crushed
2 large onions, sliced
1½ cups beef stock or broth
¾ cup dry red wine
2 tablespoons red wine vinegar
½ teaspoon dried thyme
2 tablespoons chopped parsley
¼ cup flour

Heat the oil in a deep flameproof casserole. Add the roast and brown over moderately high heat. Season with salt and pepper. Reduce heat; add the garlic and onions and cook until softened. Stir in the stock, wine, vinegar, thyme and parsley and bring to a boil. Reduce the heat, cover and simmer for 2 to 2½ hours, or until the meat is tender.

Transfer the roast to a warmed serving platter and keep hot while making the gravy.

Mix ½ cup of the pan juices with the flour, stirring until smooth. Gradually stir flour mixture into the pan and simmer over low heat, stirring until thickened.

Pour some of the gravy over roast and serve the remainder in a sauceboat. Garnish meat with chopped parsley if desired.

6 to 8 servings

Cranberry and Beef Stew

½ cup flour
1 teaspoon dried
  basil
Salt and pepper
2½ lb stewing beef,
  cut into 2-inch
  cubes
4 tablespoons oil
1½ cups beef stock
  or broth
6 whole cloves
1 stick cinnamon or
  ¼ teaspoon
  ground cinnamon
1 can (16 oz) whole
  berry cranberry
  sauce
2 tablespoons lemon
  juice
1 tablespoon butter,
  softened

Combine the flour, basil, salt and pepper and use to coat the meat. Reserve any leftover seasoned flour.

Heat the oil in a large skillet. Add the meat and brown in batches over moderately high heat. Transfer to a deep flameproof casserole.

Add the stock, cloves and cinnamon and bring to a boil. Cover and simmer over low heat for 2 hours.

Stir in the cranberry sauce and lemon juice. Cover and simmer for 20 to 30 minutes, or until the meat is tender.

Blend the butter with the remainder of the seasoned flour to make a smooth paste. Spoon a few tablespoons of the stew's cooking liquid into the paste and mix well; then stir back into the casserole and simmer, uncovered, until slightly thickened. Remove the cinnamon stick. Garnish with parsley if desired.

6 servings

Beef Teriyaki

3 lb top round steak,
  cut into
  ¼-inch-thick
  slices
¾ cup soy sauce
¾ cup sake or dry
  sherry
2 tablespoons sugar
1 clove garlic,
  crushed
2 teaspoons finely
  chopped fresh
  gingerroot

Place the beef slices between two sheets of waxed paper and pound with a wooden mallet until very thin. Arrange in a large shallow glass dish.

Combine the soy sauce, sake, sugar, garlic and ginger; pour over the meat. Marinate for at least 1 hour, turning the meat slices occasionally.

To cook, drain the meat and arrange on a rack under the broiler or over a charcoal grill. Broil or grill for about 1 minute on each side. Serve over rice.

6 servings

Stuffed Tomatoes Oriental

3 dried Chinese
  mushrooms or any
  dried wild
  mushrooms
1 tablespoon oil
1 large onion, finely
  chopped
1 lb lean ground beef
¼ cup chopped
  water chestnuts
2 tablespoons soy
  sauce
2 tablespoons dry
  sherry
8 large ripe tomatoes
1 tablespoon
  cornstarch
2 tablespoons water

Soak the mushrooms in boiling water for 15 minutes. Squeeze dry; discard the hard stems and chop the caps.

Heat the oil in a wok or large skillet. Add the onion and sauté until browned. Add the meat and sauté until evenly browned, stirring to break it up. Drain off any excess fat. Stir in the mushrooms, water chestnuts, soy sauce and sherry and simmer gently for 2 minutes.

Cut the tomatoes in half, squeezing out the seeds. Scoop out the flesh and add to the wok, reserving the tomato shells. Blend the cornstarch and water; stir into the beef and simmer, stirring, for about 1 minute. Cool slightly.

Spoon the beef mixture into the reserved shells. Arrange in a shallow non-metal baking dish. Bake in a 350° oven for 15 to 25 minutes. Garnish with coriander leaves if desired.

4 to 8 servings

Beef in Green Peppers

1 tablespoon oil
1 clove garlic,
  crushed
2 teaspoons finely
  chopped fresh
  gingerroot
½ lb lean ground
  beef
1 green onion,
  chopped
1 stalk celery, finely
  chopped
Grated rind of
  1 lemon
4 green peppers,
  seeded and cut
  into quarters

Heat the oil in a wok or large deep skillet. Add the garlic and sauté until lightly browned. Reduce the heat to moderately low, add the ginger and beef and sauté for 2 minutes, stirring to break up the meat. Add the green onion, celery and lemon rind and cook for about 30 seconds; cool slightly.

Divide the mixture among the pepper quarters, pressing it well into each cavity.

Arrange the stuffed peppers in a greased baking dish. Bake in a 400° oven for 20 to 25 minutes, or until tender. Transfer to a warmed serving platter and serve hot.

4 to 6 servings

Mustard-Glazed Picnic Ham

1 smoked picnic
  shoulder (5 to 6 lb)
2 tablespoons Dijon
  mustard
1 cup packed brown
  sugar
½ cup honey
¼ cup orange juice

Cover the ham with cold water and let soak for 3 to 4 hours. Drain and place in a roasting pan. Bake in a 325° oven for 1½ hours.

Meanwhile, prepare the glaze. In a small saucepan, combine the mustard, brown sugar, honey and orange juice. Simmer over low heat, stirring constantly, until the sugar dissolves.

Remove the ham from the oven and score the top, making diagonal cuts in the fat with a sharp knife; be careful not to cut into meat. Spoon the glaze on top. Return the ham to the oven and bake 40 to 50 minutes longer, basting occasionally.

6 servings

Pork in Applejack

½ lb bacon, diced
1½ lb stewing pork
  or shoulder, cut
  into cubes
Salt and pepper
1 lb tart apples,
  sliced
3 medium onions,
  sliced
4 large potatoes,
  thickly sliced
⅔ cup applejack
1 to 1¼ cups beef
  stock or broth
2 tablespoons butter

In a large skillet, sauté the bacon until lightly browned. Drain on paper towels and transfer to a deep casserole. Add the pork cubes to the skillet and sauté in the bacon fat over moderately high heat until browned on all sides. Transfer to the casserole and season with salt and pepper.

Arrange the sliced apples and onions in layers over the meat. Top with the potatoes. Add the applejack and just enough beef stock to cover the potatoes. Season with salt and pepper. Cover and bake in a 350° oven for 1 hour.

Remove the cover and dot the potatoes with butter. Increase the heat to 400° and bake, uncovered, for 30 minutes, or until the potatoes are golden brown.

4 servings

Ham and Kidney Beans

1 cup cubed cooked
  ham
1 can (15 oz) red
  kidney beans,
  drained
½ cup catsup
¼ cup maple syrup
1 medium onion,
  chopped
1 tablespoon cider
  vinegar
1 teaspoon dry
  mustard
¼ teaspoon ground
  cloves
Salt and pepper

Combine all the ingredients in a deep
casserole, stirring thoroughly.

    Bake uncovered in a 350° oven for 30
minutes, or until hot and bubbly.
4 servings

Roast Pork Loin in Wine

1 pork loin blade
   roast (4 lb)
4 cloves garlic,
   slivered
3 sprigs parsley
3 sprigs thyme or
   ½ teaspoon dried
1 bay leaf
Salt and pepper
¼ cup olive oil
2 cups dry white
   wine

Using a sharp knife, make small cuts in the pork around the ribs and insert the garlic. Place in a shallow glass baking dish. Add parsley, thyme and bay leaf and season with salt and pepper. Pour in the oil and wine. Cover and marinate in the refrigerator overnight, turning occasionally.

Transfer the meat to a roasting pan and pour in the marinade. Bake in a 325° oven for 2½ hours, basting occasionally with cooking liquid.

Transfer the roast to a warmed serving platter and keep hot. Strain the cooking liquid into a small saucepan and skim off the fat. Boil over high heat to reduce and thicken slightly. Adjust the seasoning and pour over roast, or pass in a sauceboat. Garnish the roast with fresh herbs if desired.

6 servings

Pork Cutlets with Prunes

½ lb pitted prunes
⅔ cup medium-dry
  sherry
⅔ cup water
4 pork cutlets
Salt and pepper
1½ tablespoons
  flour
¾ cup heavy cream
1 tablespoon currant
  jelly

Soak the prunes in a bowl with the sherry and water overnight. Drain, reserving the liquid.

Pound the cutlets with a wooden mallet to flatten. Season both sides with salt and pepper. Place a layer of prunes on top of each cutlet. Starting with the short end, roll up each cutlet and tie with string.

Place the cutlets in a small roasting pan and pour the reserved liquid over. Bake in a 350° oven, basting occasionally, for about 45 to 50 minutes, or until the pork is cooked through.

Transfer the pork rolls to a warmed serving platter. Skim off any fat from the cooking liquid. Blend the flour with the cream and gradually stir into the cooking liquid. Simmer gently until thickened. Stir in the currant jelly. Adjust the seasoning.

Serve the pork with the sauce. Garnish with watercress if desired.

4 servings

Pork with Apple and Ginger: Substitute 2 apples, chopped, and ¼ cup raisins for prunes. Add ½ teaspoon ground cinnamon and ¼ teaspoon ground ginger to the sherry and water mixture. Divide the apple mixture among the 4 cutlets, roll up and proceed as directed above.

Pork with Tangy Apricot Stuffing: Substitute ½ lb dried apricots for the prunes. Add 2 tablespoons brown sugar and 2 tablespoons soy sauce to the sherry and water mixture and proceed as directed above. Substitute 2 tablespoons apricot preserve for the currant jelly.

Country Veal Casserole

2 tablespoons oil
1¼ lb stewing veal or
   shoulder, cut in
   1-inch cubes
1 onion, sliced
2 stalks celery,
   chopped
1 green pepper,
   seeded and
   chopped
2 tablespoons flour
1¼ cups apple juice
1¼ cups chicken
   stock or broth
¼ cup raisins
¼ cup chopped
   walnuts
⅓ cup dried apricots
Salt and pepper
⅔ cup sour cream
⅔ cup grated
   Cheddar cheese

Heat the oil in a large skillet. Add the veal and sauté over moderately high heat until evenly browned. Transfer to a 2½-quart casserole.

Add the onion, celery and green pepper to the skillet and sauté for about 1 minute. Stir in the flour and cook for 1 minute. Gradually stir in the apple juice and stock and continue to simmer, stirring, over moderately low heat until the sauce thickens. Add the raisins, walnuts and apricots. Simmer for 2 minutes and pour over the veal. Cover and bake in a 325° oven for 2 hours.

Season to taste with salt and pepper and spoon the sour cream over the veal. Sprinkle with the cheese. Return the casserole to the oven, uncovered, for 10 minutes. Serve with rice.

4 servings

Nutty Chicken Bake

8 chicken parts,
  skinned
1 medium onion,
  sliced
¼ cup salted peanuts
1 can (10¾ oz)
  condensed cream
  of celery soup
⅔ cup milk
½ cup grated
  Monterey Jack
  cheese
⅓ cup bread crumbs

Arrange the chicken parts in a 2-quart casserole and sprinkle with the onion and half of the peanuts. Blend the soup and milk and pour over the chicken. Cover and bake in a 350° oven for 1¼ hours.

Crush or finely chop the remaining peanuts and mix with the cheese and bread crumbs. Sprinkle the mixture over the chicken. Return to the oven, uncovered, for 20 minutes, or until the topping is crisp and golden. Garnish with parsley if desired.

4 servings

Southern Fried Chicken

½ cup flour
Salt and pepper
1 to 1½ teaspoons
    grated nutmeg
1 chicken (2½ to
    3 lb), cut into
    8 pieces
½ cup milk
Oil for frying

Season the flour with a little salt, a generous amount of pepper and the nutmeg. Dip the chicken into the milk, then dredge in the flour. Dip again in milk and dredge in flour.

Pour oil into a 10- to 12-inch skillet to a depth of about 1 inch. Heat the oil until hot. Carefully add the chicken pieces and fry, turning once, for 20 minutes, or until the chicken is fork tender. Drain well. Garnish with parsley if desired.

4 servings

Chicken Pot Pie

4 tablespoon butter
6 tablespoons flour
⅔ cup milk
1¼ cups chicken stock or broth
3 cups diced cooked chicken
¼ lb mushrooms, chopped
½ green pepper, seeded and chopped
1 tablespoon chopped parsley
½ teaspoon celery salt
Salt and pepper
1 sheet (5 × 10 inches) puff pastry, thawed
1 egg, beaten

In a large saucepan, melt the butter. Stir in the flour and cook, stirring, over moderate heat for about 1 minute. Gradually stir in the milk and stock and bring to a boil, stirring constantly. Add the chicken, mushrooms, green pepper and parsley. Season with the celery salt, salt and pepper. Transfer to a 1½-quart casserole.

Roll out the puff pastry to 1 inch larger than the casserole top. Cut off a ½-inch strip all around pastry and place on the dampened rim of the casserole. Dampen the top of the strip with water. Position the puff pastry over the casserole, pressing the edge down. Trim and flute the edge and cut an air vent in the center. Decorate with pastry leaves if desired.

Brush the pastry with the beaten egg. Bake in a 425° oven for 30 minutes, or until golden brown.

4 to 6 servings

Broiled Deviled Chicken

2 tablespoons Dijon
  mustard
2 tablespoons
  prepared English
  mustard
¼ cup sugar
4 tablespoons lemon
  juice
2 tablespoons oil
2 teaspoons
  Worcestershire
  sauce
Salt and pepper
1 chicken (2½ to
  3 lb), cut into
  8 pieces

In a small bowl, combine the mustards, sugar, lemon juice, oil, Worcestershire and salt and pepper.

Arrange the chicken pieces in a broiler pan. Spoon about a fourth of the sauce over the chicken and broil about 4 inches from the heat for 15 minutes, brushing more sauce over chicken midway through cooking. Turn the chicken and brush with sauce. Cook for 15 minutes longer, or until fork tender, brushing with the remaining sauce midway through cooking.

Serve hot, on a bed of lettuce leaves if desired.

4 servings

Orange-Baked Chicken

4 tablespoons butter
1 tablespoon oil
1 chicken (2½ to
  3 lb), cut into
  8 pieces
2 medium onions,
  finely chopped
2 tablespoons
  Worcestershire
  sauce
2 tablespoons water
1 tablespoon tomato
  paste
Grated rind of
  1 orange
Rind of 1 orange, cut
  into thin strips
Juice of 2 oranges
Salt and pepper

In a large skillet, melt the butter in the oil. Add the chicken pieces and sauté over moderately high heat until brown on both sides. Transfer to a baking dish. Add the onions to the skillet and sauté over low heat for about 5 minutes. Add the onions to the casserole and drain any remaining fat from the skillet.

Add the Worcestershire sauce, water, tomato paste, orange rind (grated and strips) and juice to the skillet. Bring to a boil and season with salt and pepper.

Spoon the sauce over the chicken. Cover and bake in a 350° oven for 1 hour.

To serve, transfer chicken to a warmed serving platter and spoon sauce over. Serve remaining sauce in a sauceboat.

4 servings

Chicken and Raisin Casserole

½ cup flour
Salt and pepper
Grated nutmeg
1 chicken (2½ to
  3 lb), cut into
  8 pieces
½ cup butter
2 tablespoons oil
2 medium onions,
  chopped
4 slices bacon, diced
2½ cups chicken
  stock or broth
½ lb mushrooms,
  sliced
4 medium tomatoes,
  chopped
¾ cup golden raisins

Season the flour with salt, pepper and nutmeg and use to coat the chicken pieces. Reserve any leftover seasoned flour.

In a large skillet, melt the butter in the oil. Add the chicken and sauté, turning frequently, for about 10 minutes, or until golden brown all over. Transfer to a baking dish.

Add the onions and bacon to the skillet and sauté until the onions are softened. Sprinkle in any remaining flour and cook, stirring, for 1 minute. Gradually add the stock and bring to a boil over high heat, stirring.

Pour the sauce over the chicken in the casserole. Add the mushrooms, tomatoes and raisins. Cover and bake in a 350° oven for 1 hour, or until fork tender.

4 servings

Barbecued Chicken

¼ cup currant jelly
¼ cup lemon juice
¼ cup oil
¼ cup chicken stock
   or broth
½ teaspoon dry
   mustard
½ teaspoon
   Worcestershire
   sauce
Salt and pepper
1 chicken (2½ to
   3 lb), cut into
   8 pieces

Melt the jelly in a small saucepan. Stir in the lemon juice, oil, stock, mustard and Worcestershire; season with salt and pepper.

Arrange the chicken pieces in one layer in a shallow glass dish and pour the jelly mixture over them. Cover and marinate in the refrigerator overnight.

Drain the chicken pieces, reserving the marinade. Place the chicken pieces skin-side down on a broiler pan about 4 inches from the heat. Broil for 10 minutes. Turn and baste with the marinade. Broil 10 minutes longer, or until the chicken is fork tender and the skin is crisp.

4 servings

44

Mandarin Chicken Breasts

3 whole chicken
  breasts, split and
  skinned
3 tablespoons butter,
  melted
1 can (11 oz)
  mandarin oranges
1¼ cup chicken
  stock or broth
1 tablespoon
  cornstarch
½ teaspoon curry
  powder
½ tablespoon lemon
  juice
Salt and pepper
¼ cup finely
  chopped onion
1 medium green
  pepper, seeded and
  thinly sliced
¼ lb pitted dates,
  halved

Brush the breasts all over with melted butter. Arrange in one layer in a baking dish and pour any remaining butter over. Bake in a 350° oven for 1 hour, or until cooked through.

Meanwhile, drain the mandarin oranges, reserving ⅔ cup syrup. (If there isn't enough, add stock.)

In a small saucepan, combine the reserved syrup and the stock. Blend the cornstarch with 2 tablespoons of the stock mixture and stir into the saucepan. Add the curry powder and lemon juice and season with salt and pepper. Bring to a boil. Reduce heat and simmer, stirring, until the mixture thickens. Add the onion and green pepper and simmer for 5 minutes, or until the vegetables are tender. Stir in the oranges and dates. Pour the sauce over the chicken breasts.

6 servings

FISH

Tuna Cakes

2 large potatoes,
  cooked
2 tablespoons butter
1 can (13 oz) tuna,
  drained and flaked
2 tablespoons
  chopped parsley
2 eggs, beaten
  separately
Salt and pepper
1 cup dry bread
  crumbs
¼ cup oil

In a bowl, mash the potatoes with the butter. Add the tuna, parsley, 1 beaten egg and salt and pepper to taste; mix well. Chill for 30 minutes.

On a floured surface, shape the tuna mixture into a roll about 2½ inches in diameter. Cut into 8 slices; shape each into a flat round. Dip each in the remaining beaten egg, then coat evenly with bread crumbs.

Heat the oil in a large skillet. Add the fish cakes and fry for 2 to 3 minutes on each side, or until golden brown and heated through.

4 servings

Cheesy Broiled Cod

4 cod steaks, about
 1 inch thick
¾ cup grated
 Cheddar cheese
1 teaspoon
 Worcestershire
 sauce
1 tablespoon milk
Salt and pepper

Place the steaks on a greased broiler pan and broil on one side for 4 to 5 minutes.

Meanwhile, combine the cheese, Worcestershire and milk; season with salt and pepper.

Turn the fish and spread the uncooked side with the cheese mixture. Broil for about 5 minutes, until the fish is cooked and the cheese topping is golden brown and bubbling. Garnish with parsley if desired.

4 servings

Cod Steaks and Tomatoes

4 cod steaks, about
  1 inch thick
½ lb mushrooms,
  sliced
4 tomatoes, sliced
1 clove garlic,
  crushed (optional)
2 tablespoons dry
  white wine
1 tablespoon lemon
  juice
Salt and pepper

Place the cod steaks in a well-greased baking dish. Top with the mushrooms, tomatoes and garlic. Add the wine and lemon juice and season with salt and pepper.

Cover with foil and bake in a 350° oven for 30 minutes. Garnish with chopped parsley if desired.
4 servings

Baked Flounder and Spinach

1½ lb fresh spinach
  or 2 packages
  (10 oz) frozen
  spinach, cooked
  and finely
  chopped
3 tablespoons
  half-and-half
2 tablespoons butter,
  melted
Salt and pepper
Grated nutmeg
8 small flounder
  fillets
2 tablespoons grated
  Parmesan cheese

Thoroughly combine the cooked spinach, half-and-half, butter and season with salt, pepper and nutmeg. Spread in the bottom of a well-greased baking dish.

Roll up the fish fillets lengthwise and secure with wooden picks. Arrange them on the spinach bed and sprinkle with Parmesan. Cover and bake in a 350° oven for 30 minutes. Garnish with tomato wedges or slices if desired.
4 servings

Whiting in Oatmeal

4 whole whiting,
  cleaned
Salt and pepper
⅔ cup oatmeal
2 tablespoons butter
1 tablespoon oil

Rub the fish with a little salt. Rinse and pat dry. Season with salt and pepper.

Coat the fish well with the oatmeal, pressing firmly in place. Melt the butter in the oil in a large skillet. Add the fish and sauté for 8 minutes, turning once. Drain and serve with lemon wedges.
4 servings

Fish and Tomato Bake

4 tablespoons butter
4 slices bacon, diced
2 medium onions,
  finely chopped
4 tomatoes, chopped
1 clove garlic,
  crushed (optional)
Salt and pepper
1 tablespoon
  chopped parsley
4 haddock or cod
  fillets
1 tablespoon lemon
  juice
1 cup bread crumbs
½ cup grated
  Parmesan cheese

Melt the butter in a large skillet. Add the bacon, onions, tomatoes and garlic and sauté until the onions are softened. Season with salt and pepper. Transfer the mixture to a well-greased casserole. Sprinkle with the parsley. Arrange the fish fillets on top of the vegetables and sprinkle with the lemon juice.

Combine the bread crumbs and cheese and sprinkle evenly over the fish. Bake in a 325° oven for 30 minutes, or until the fish is tender and the topping is golden brown.

4 servings

Fish Baked in Cider

1 medium onion,
  finely chopped
¼ lb mushrooms,
  chopped
4 halibut or cod
  steaks, about 1
  inch thick
1 egg, beaten
3 tablespoons bread
  crumbs
2 teaspoons lemon
  juice
Salt and pepper
¼ cup hard cider
2 tablespoons butter

Spread the onion and mushrooms in the bottom of a shallow baking dish.

Dip the fish steaks into the egg; then coat well on both sides with the bread crumbs. Arrange the steaks on top of the vegetables and sprinkle with the lemon juice. Season with salt and pepper. Spoon the cider over the fish and dot with the butter.

Bake in a 325° oven for 40 minutes, or until the fish is tender. Garnish with chopped parsley if desired.

4 servings

Mustard-Marinated Halibut

6 halibut steaks
6 tablespoons oil
3 tablespoons lemon
  juice
2 teaspoons Meaux
  or other
  coarse-grained
  mustard
Salt and pepper
2 tablespoons butter
1 medium onion,
  finely chopped
⅔ cup bread crumbs
¼ cup grated
  Parmesan cheese
2 tablespoons
  chopped parsley

Arrange the halibut steaks in one layer in a shallow dish. Combine the oil, lemon juice and mustard, salt and pepper and pour over the fish. Allow to marinate for at least 30 minutes, turning occasionally.

Meanwhile, melt the butter in a medium skillet. Add the onion and sauté until softened. Stir in the bread crumbs, cheese and parsley.

Drain the fish steaks and arrange in a baking dish. Spread the crumb mixture over the fish. Bake in a 350° oven for 30 minutes.

6 servings

Sole Baked in Sour Cream

1 tablespoon butter
3 lb sole fillets, cut
  into strips
Juice of ½ lemon
Salt and pepper
1 tablespoon dried
  tarragon
2 cups sour cream
2 teaspoons chopped
  parsley

Grease a large shallow baking dish with the butter. Arrange the fillets in one layer in the dish. Sprinkle with the lemon juice and season with salt, pepper and tarragon. Spoon the sour cream over the fish.

Bake in a 350° oven for 25 minutes, or until the fish is cooked through. Serve garnished with the parsley.

6 servings

Salmon Steaks in Vermouth

⅓ cup bread crumbs
Salt and pepper
4 salmon steaks
4 tablespoons butter
2 teaspoons lemon
  juice
4 tablespoons dry
  vermouth

Season the bread crumbs with salt and pepper and coat the salmon.

In a large skillet, melt the butter over moderate heat. Add the salmon and brown on both sides. Transfer the fish to a baking dish and pour the butter in the skillet over the fish. Sprinkle with lemon juice and vermouth.

Bake in a 375° oven for 20 minutes.

4 servings

VEGETABLES & SALADS

Zucchini and Tomatoes

4 tablespoons butter
2 tablespoons olive oil
4 medium zucchini, sliced
4 large tomatoes, chopped
2 cloves garlic, crushed (optional)
Salt and pepper

Melt the butter in the oil in a large skillet. Add the zucchini and sauté over moderate heat until golden brown on both sides. Add the tomatoes and garlic and season with salt and pepper. Continue to sauté, gently mixing vegetables together, until the tomatoes are tender.

4 servings

Glazed Carrots

1 lb carrots
1 chicken or beef
  bouillon cube
1 tablespoon sugar
4 tablespoons butter

If the carrots are small and tender, leave them whole. Cut larger carrots into 2-inch lengths.

Place the carrots in a large saucepan with just enough water to come up to the level of the carrots. Bring to a boil over moderately high heat and add the bouillon cube, sugar and butter. Reduce heat, cover and simmer for 10 minutes.

Remove the cover and continue cooking for another 10 to 15 minutes, or until the carrots are cooked and the water has nearly evaporated. Drain and serve, sprinkled with chopped parsley if desired.

4 servings

Cauliflower in Cheese Sauce

1 medium head
  cauliflower, cut
  into flowerets
6 tablespoons butter
2 medium onions,
  chopped
4 slices bacon, diced
4 tablespoons flour
1 ¼ cups milk
1 cup grated Cheddar
  cheese
1 tablespoon oil
¼ lb mushrooms,
  chopped
Salt and pepper

Cook the cauliflower in boiling salted water for 5 to 10 minutes, or until just tender. Drain thoroughly.

Melt 3 tablespoons of the butter in a medium saucepan. Add the onions and bacon and sauté gently 5 minutes. Stir in the flour and cook, stirring, for 1 minute. Gradually stir in the milk and and bring to a boil, stirring constantly. Cook, stirring, for 2 minutes. Remove from the heat and stir in all but 1 tablespoon of the cheese.

Melt the remaining butter in the oil in a medium skillet. Add the mushrooms and sauté over moderately high heat. Drain the mushrooms of excess butter and stir them into the sauce. Season with salt and pepper.

Arrange the cauliflower in a warmed flameproof dish and pour the sauce on top. Sprinkle with the reserved cheese and broil until the top is golden brown.

4 servings

Beef-Stuffed Zucchini

2 to 3 large zucchini
4 tablespoons butter
2 tablespoons oil
1 medium onion,
  finely chopped
4 slices bacon, diced
1 clove garlic,
  crushed (optional)
½ lb lean ground
  beef
¼ cup bread crumbs
2 tomatoes, peeled
  and chopped
½ teaspoon mixed
  dried herbs
Salt and pepper
Grated nutmeg

Using a sharp chef's knife, cut the zucchini crosswise into 2-inch slices, trimming the ends. Use a melon baller or small spoon to scoop out a hollow in each slice. Place the slices hollow side up in a large, well-greased shallow baking dish.

In a large skillet, melt 2 tablespoons of the butter in the oil. Add the onion, bacon and garlic and sauté gently until softened. Add the beef, increase the heat to moderate and cook, stirring to break up meat, until evenly browned. Remove from the heat, drain off excess fat and mix in bread crumbs, tomatoes and herbs. Season with salt and pepper.

Season the zucchini with salt, pepper and nutmeg. Spoon the beef into each slice, pressing it gently into the hollow and mounding it on top. Dot with the remaining butter. Cover with foil and bake in a 350° oven for 35 minutes, or until bubbling.

4 servings

Skillet Potatoes and Onions

4 medium onions,
  thinly sliced
Salt and pepper
4 to 6 medium
  potatoes, cut into
  ¼-inch slices
2 cups beef stock or
  broth

Arrange the onion rings in the bottom of a large skillet and season with salt and pepper. Arrange the potato slices in layers on top of the onions. Season with salt and pepper.

Add the stock, cover and simmer for 20 to 30 minutes, or until the vegetables are tender.

4 servings

Cauliflower Puree

1 medium head
  cauliflower, cut
  into flowerets
2 tablespoons butter
4 tablespoons flour
1¼ cups milk
Salt and pepper
Grated nutmeg

Cook the cauliflower in boiling salted water for 5 to 10 minutes, or until tender. Drain thoroughly.

Melt the butter in a small saucepan. Stir in the flour and cook, stirring, for 1 minute. Gradually stir in the milk; bring to a boil, stirring constantly. Season with salt, pepper and nutmeg and cook, stirring, for 2 minutes longer.

Transfer the cauliflower to a food processor, blender or food mill and puree. Stir the puree into the white sauce and blend until smooth. Heat through; then spoon into a warmed vegetable dish and sprinkle with additional nutmeg if desired.

4 servings

NOTE: Vegetable purees are becoming more popular. Consider the stuffed zucchini on page 57. It could just as well be stuffed with a vegetable puree as with beef. Cook the zucchini and puree separately. To serve, spoon the puree into the zucchini and heat briefly. You will need about a pound to a pound and a half of vegetables for the amount of white sauce given the in the recipe above.

Buttered Leeks

6 to 8 leeks, sliced
  and rinsed
4 tablespoons butter
Salt and pepper
Grated nutmeg

In a medium saucepan, cook the leeks in boiling salted water for 10 minutes. Drain well and rinse saucepan. Melt the butter in the saucepan. Return the leeks to the pan and toss well in the butter. Season with salt, pepper and nutmeg.

4 servings

Rutabaga with Bacon

1 medium rutabaga,
   cut into 1-inch
   cubes
4 slices bacon, diced
2 tablespoons butter
Salt and pepper
Grated nutmeg
2 tablespoons milk
   or half-and-half

In a large saucepan, cook the rutabaga in boiling salted water for about 30 minutes, or until tender.

Meanwhile, fry the bacon in a medium skillet until crisp.

Drain the cubed rutabaga thoroughly. Transfer to a food processor, blender or food mill and puree. Return the puree to the saucepan and stir in the butter and bacon. Season to taste with salt, pepper and nutmeg. Stir in the milk and heat through.

This dish is delicious with roast pork.

4 servings

Potato Pancakes

4 medium potatoes,
  grated
2 eggs, beaten
Salt and pepper
2 tablespoons
  chopped parsley
1 small onion, grated
  (optional)
½ cup shredded
  Cheddar cheese
  (optional)
Oil for frying

Drain the grated potatoes on paper towels. Season the eggs with salt, pepper and chopped parsley and stir in the potatoes, onion and cheese.

In a large skillet, heat a few tablespoons of oil until hot. For each pancake, spoon about 2 tablespoons of the mixture into the pan and flatten lightly. Cook for about 4 minutes on each side, or until golden brown.

Transfer to a warmed serving platter and keep warm. Repeat with the remaining mixture. Serve with applesauce if desired.

6 to 8 servings

Camembert-Topped Leeks

1½ lb leeks, cut in
   half lengthwise
   and rinsed
2 tablespoons butter
1 tablespoon finely
   chopped onion
4 tablespoons flour
1¼ cups milk
¼ lb Camembert
   cheese (rind
   removed),
   chopped
1 hard-cooked egg,
   finely chopped
Salt and pepper

Cook the leeks in a large pan of boiling
salted water for about 8 minutes, or
until tender. Drain and arrange in a
shallow baking dish; keep warm while
preparing the sauce.

Melt the butter in a small saucepan.
Add the onion and sauté until softened. Stir in the flour and cook for
1 minute. Gradually stir in the milk
and simmer, stirring, until the sauce
thickens. Add the cheese and egg and
season with salt and pepper. Simmer
gently for 1 minute longer.

Pour the sauce over the leeks and
serve. Garnish with chopped parsley if
desired.

4 servings

Zucchini-Tomato Gratin

1 tablespoon butter
1 large onion, sliced
1 clove garlic, crushed
4 medium zucchini, peeled, halved lengthwise and cut into 1-inch pieces
1 can (14½ oz) whole tomatoes
1 teaspoon each dried basil and oregano
Salt and pepper
¾ cup grated Cheddar cheese
¼ cup grated Gruyère cheese
1 cup bread crumbs

Melt the butter in a large saucepan. Add the onion and garlic and sauté until softened. Add the zucchini, the tomatoes with their juice, basil and oregano, and season with salt and pepper. Bring to a boil; reduce heat, cover and simmer for 10 minutes, or until the zucchini is tender. Transfer to a shallow flameproof casserole.

Combine the cheeses and bread crumbs and sprinkle over the vegetables. Place under the broiler for 2 to 3 minutes, or until the topping is golden brown. Serve immediately.

4 servings

Beany Cheese Crunch

⅓ cup dried kidney beans
⅓ cup dried black-eyed peas
⅓ cup dried lima beans
2 tablespoons oil
1 large onion, finely chopped
2 stalks celery, finely chopped
4 slices bacon, chopped
1 clove garlic, crushed
1 can (14½ oz) whole tomatoes
⅔ cup chicken stock or broth
¼ teaspoon chili powder
Salt and pepper
1 cup bread crumbs
1 cup grated sharp Cheddar cheese

Soak the kidney beans, black-eyed peas and lima beans in cold water overnight. Drain and place in a saucepan. Cover with cold water and bring to a boil over high heat; boil rapidly for 10 minutes. Reduce the heat, cover and simmer for 30 to 35 minutes, or until tender.

Meanwhile, heat the oil in a large skillet. Add the onion, celery, bacon and garlic and sauté until softened. Stir in the tomatoes and their juice and the stock. Add the chili powder and season with salt and pepper.

Drain the beans and rinse under cold water. Add them to the tomato mixture and bring to a boil. Reduce the heat, cover and simmer for 20 minutes. Transfer the bean mixture to a 1½-quart flameproof casserole.

Combine the breadcrumbs and cheese and sprinkle over the bean mixture. Place under the broiler until the topping is golden brown. Serve hot.
4 servings

Vegetable Stew and Dumplings

1 onion
½ lb carrots
4 tomatoes, peeled
1 small cauliflower
1 tablespoon oil
1¼ cups chicken
  stock or broth
1 tablespoon tomato
  paste
1½ teaspoons dried
  mixed herbs
Salt and pepper
½ cup each frozen
  green beans and
  peas
½ cup unsalted
  peanuts
½ cup flour
¾ teaspoon baking
  powder
¼ teaspoon salt
2 tablespoons
  shortening
¾ cup grated
  Cheddar cheese

Slice the onion and carrots. Chop the tomatoes. Divide the cauliflower into flowerets.

Heat the oil in a large saucepan. Add the onion and carrots and sauté for 5 minutes. Stir in the tomatoes, stock, tomato paste, 1 teaspoon of the dried herbs and season with salt and pepper. Bring to a boil. Reduce heat, cover and simmer for 15 minutes. Add the cauliflower, beans, peas and nuts and simmer for 15 minutes.

Meanwhile, prepare the dumplings. Combine the flour, baking powder, salt, shortening, remaining herbs and ¼ cup of the cheese in a mixing bowl. Season with salt and pepper. Stir in 4 tablespoons of water to make an elastic dough. Turn onto a floured surface and form into 8 balls.

Place the dumplings on top of the vegetables. Sprinkle with the remaining cheese. Cover and simmer over moderately low heat for 30 minutes.

4 servings

Basic Fritter Batter

1 cup flour
Pinch of salt
⅔ cup milk
1 egg yolk
2 tablespoons butter,
  melted
2 egg whites, stiffly
  beaten

In a mixing bowl, combine the flour and salt and make a well in the center. Pour half of the milk and the egg yolk into the well. Using a spoon, gradually incorporate the flour into the liquid. When the mixture becomes very stiff, add the remaining milk gradually, beating well between each addition to make a thick batter. Stir in the melted butter and carefully fold in the egg whites.

Makes about 1¼ cups batter

Corn Fritters

2 eggs, separated
2 tablespoons flour
1 can (12 oz) whole
  kernel corn,
  drained
Salt and pepper
2 tablespoons butter
  or bacon drippings
  for frying

Mix together the egg yolks, flour and corn. Season with salt and pepper. Beat the egg whites until stiff and fold them into the corn mixture.

Heat the butter until sizzling in a large heavy-bottomed skillet. Spoon in the batter by tablespoons. Fry until set and lightly browned. Turn the fritters carefully with a spatula and brown the other side. Drain on paper towels and serve immediately.

12 to 14 fritters

Turnip Fritters

3 medium white
  turnips, cut
  lengthwise into
  ¼-inch slices
1¼ cups fritter
  batter
Oil for deep-frying

Dip the turnip slices into the fritter batter and coat them thoroughly.

Heat the oil in the deep fryer to 350° to 365°, or until a bread cube dropped into the oil browns in 60 seconds. Slip the turnip slices, a few at a time, into the oil, frying for about 5 minutes, or until crisp and golden.

Drain well on paper towels and keep hot in a 425° oven while frying the remaining turnips.

16 to 18 fritters

Deep-Fried Onion Rings

2 large onions, cut
    into ¼-inch slices
1¼ cups fritter
    batter
Oil for deep-frying

Separate the onion slices into rings. Drop the rings, a few at a time, into a small mixing bowl filled with fritter batter and lift them out with a skewer.

Heat the oil in a deep fryer to 350° to 365°, or until a cube of bread dropped into the oil browns in 60 seconds. Slip onion rings, a few at a time, into the oil and fry for 2 to 3 minutes, or until crisp and browned.

Drain thoroughly on paper towels and keep hot in a 425° oven while frying the remaining onions.

4 to 6 servings

Deep-Fried Parsley: Separate into sprigs and wash. Pat dry, making sure no water clings to the leaves. Dip into batter and slip into the oil. Fry until browned.

67

Chinese Cabbage

1 head Chinese
   cabbage, shredded
4 tablespoons butter
Grated rind and juice
   of 1 orange
½ teaspoon grated
   nutmeg

Boil the cabbage in a small amount of salted water for about 5 minutes. Drain well.

Melt the butter in a large saucepan. Add the orange rind, orange juice, nutmeg and cabbage; toss well. Serve garnished with chopped parsley if desired.
6 servings

Nutty Potatoes

2 lb potatoes, cooked
   and mashed
4 tablespoons butter
2 tablespoons milk
1 cup chopped mixed
   nuts

In a medium mixing bowl, combine the mashed potatoes, butter and milk. Shape the mixture into a long roll and cut into 24 pieces. Roll each piece into a ball; then flatten into cakes. Coat with the chopped nuts.

Arrange the cakes on a greased baking sheet and bake in a 350° oven for 20 minutes, or until crisp and golden.
6 servings

Spinach Cannelloni

2 packages (10 oz each) frozen chopped spinach, thawed and squeezed dry
1½ cups grated sharp Cheddar cheese
⅔ cup bread crumbs
Salt and pepper
Grated nutmeg
8 lasagne noodles
2 tablespoons butter
2 tablespoons flour
1¼ cups milk
1 teaspoon prepared mustard

In a mixing bowl, combine the spinach with ¼ cup of the cheese and 3 tablespoons of the bread crumbs. Season with salt, pepper and nutmeg.

Cook the lasagne in boiling salted water for 15 minutes, or until just tender. Drain and rinse with cold water. Cut each noodle in half crosswise and lay out flat on a clean kitchen towel. Divide the spinach mixture among the noodles and roll each up jelly-roll fashion. Place the rolls, seam side down, in a greased shallow baking dish.

Melt the butter in a small saucepan. Stir in the flour and cook for 1 minute. Gradually stir in the milk and simmer, stirring, until the sauce thickens. Add ⅓ cup of the remaining cheese and the mustard and season to taste with salt and pepper.

Pour the sauce over the cannelloni. Combine the remaining bread crumbs and cheese and sprinkle over the sauce.

Bake in a 375° oven for 20 to 30 minutes, or until the topping is golden.
4 servings

Fruit and Ham Salad

1 head lettuce
2 large oranges,
  peeled, sectioned
  and cut into
  1-inch pieces
½ cucumber, peeled
  and diced
1 green pepper,
  chopped
½ lb seedless grapes
4 thin slices cooked
  ham
⅔ cup French
  dressing
  (see page 81)

Line a large salad bowl with a layer of lettuce leaves. Arrange the oranges, cucumber, pepper and grapes in layers on top of the lettuce. Continue to layer lettuce, fruits and vegetables in this fashion until all have been used.

Roll up the ham slices and arrange on top of the salad. Serve the French dressing separately.

4 servings

Carrot and Apple Slaw

2 apples, peeled and
  sliced
Juice of 1 lemon
½ head cabbage,
  shredded
½ lb carrots,
  shredded
½ teaspoon dried
  oregano
⅔ cup French
  dressing
  (see page 81)

Combine the apples and lemon juice in the bottom of a large salad bowl and toss to coat the apples well. Add the cabbage and carrots and toss.

Add the oregano to the dressing and pour over the salad. Toss.

4 servings

Sliced Tomatoes and Cucumbers

6 to 8 ripe tomatoes,
  sliced
½ to 1 cucumber,
  peeled and sliced
Salt and pepper
1 teaspoon sugar
⅔ cup French
  dressing
  (see page 81)
½ teaspoon dried
  marjoram

Arrange the tomato and cucumber slices in layers in a shallow serving dish. Season with the salt, pepper and sugar. Let stand for at least 10 minutes.

Pour the French dressing over the salad and sprinkle with marjoram. This salad makes a delicious accompaniment to broiled meats.

4 servings

Warm Potato Salad

4 medium potatoes,
    quartered
3 eggs
1 clove garlic,
    crushed
2 medium onions,
    chopped
1 small green pepper,
    seeded and finely
    chopped
1 to 2 tablespoons
    chopped chives or
    green onion tops
1 tablespoon
    chopped parsley
1½ tablespoons
    cider vinegar or
    lemon juice
1 teaspoon
    horseradish sauce
Freshly ground black
    pepper

Cook the potatoes in a lightly salted boiling water for about 20 minutes, or until tender. Simmer the eggs for about 12 minutes to hard cook.

Meanwhile, rub the inside of a large salad or serving bowl with the crushed garlic; discard garlic. Combine the onions, green pepper, chives, parsley, vinegar and horseradish sauce in the bowl.

Dice the potatoes and shell and dice the eggs while still warm. Add to the bowl, season with the ground pepper and toss all ingredients lightly. Serve while still warm, accompanied with mayonnaise.

4 servings

Confetti Rice Salad

1 cup rice, cooked
1 green pepper,
   seeded and
   chopped
½ lb tomatoes,
   peeled and
   chopped
1 can (16 oz) whole
   kernel corn,
   drained
2 tablespoons golden
   raisins
1 small onion, finely
   chopped
2 stalks celery, finely
   chopped
2 tablespoons
   chopped parsley
French dressing
   (see page 81)
Salt and pepper

In a large salad or serving bowl, combine the rice, green pepper, tomatoes, corn, raisins, onion, celery and parsley.

Add enough French dressing to moisten the salad, season with the salt and pepper and toss well. Serve with cold chicken or ham.

4 servings

73

New Potato Salad

1 lb small new
  potatoes, cooked,
  peeled and thinly
  sliced
¼ lb salami, diced
2 stalks celery,
  chopped
1 tablespoon
  chopped chives or
  green onion tops
1 tablespoon
  chopped parsley
6 to 8 tablespoons
  mayonnaise
4 hard-cooked eggs

Combine the potatoes, salami, celery, chives, parsley and mayonnaise in a large mixing bowl.

Cut the eggs in half, remove the yolks and force them through a sieve. Add half of the yolks to the potato mixture; reserve the other half for garnishing. Chop the egg whites and add to the potatoes.

Toss the ingredients gently, mixing well without breaking the potatoes.

If desired, serve on a bed of watercress, garnished with the reserved egg yolk and paprika.

4 to 6 servings

Salami and Egg Salad

3 eggs, lightly scrambled

1 can (7 oz) whole kernel corn, drained

4 tablespoons mayonnaise

8 thin slices large salami

1 head lettuce, shredded

2 to 3 leaves red cabbage, finely shredded

2 tablespoons French dressing (see page 81)

In a mixing bowl, combine the eggs, corn and mayonnaise.

Cut a large wedge, or about one quarter of each round, out of the salami slices and cut the wedges into matchstick strips. Place them in a serving dish with the lettuce and red cabbage. Spoon the French dressing over the shredded greens and salami strips and toss lightly.

Roll up the salami slices into cones and fill each with the egg and corn mixture. Arrange the salami cones, seam sides down, on the bed of greens in the serving dish. Garnish with watercress if desired.

4 servings

Green Salad and Roquefort

1 small head
   romaine lettuce
½ cucumber, sliced
2 stalks celery,
   chopped
1 head curly endive,
   shredded
¾ cup crumbled
   Roquefort or blue
   cheese
2 tablespoons milk
⅔ cup sour cream
Salt and pepper

Tear the romaine into pieces in a large salad bowl. Add the cucumber, celery and endive; toss well.

Place the cheese in a shallow bowl; add the milk and mash together with a fork until the mixture is smooth. Blend in the sour cream and season to taste with salt and pepper.

Pour the dressing over the salad just before serving and toss.

4 servings

Cheesy Chicken Salad

½ lb cooked
   chicken, cut into
   1-inch cubes
¼ lb Swiss cheese,
   cut into thin strips
½ lb bean sprouts
1 green pepper,
   seeded and sliced
1 tablespoon finely
   chopped onion
2-inch length of
   cucumber, cut
   into strips
4 tablespoons plain
   yogurt
4 tablespoons
   mayonnaise
1 clove garlic,
   pressed
1 teaspoon ground
   coriander
1 tablespoon soy
   sauce
Salt and pepper

In a large mixing bowl, combine the chicken, cheese, bean sprouts, green pepper, onion and cucumber.

In another small bowl, combine the yogurt, mayonnaise, garlic, coriander and soy sauce and season with salt and pepper to taste. Pour the dressing over the chicken mixture and toss well. Transfer to a serving bowl.

4 servings

Crispy Bacon Salad

¼ lb smoked bacon,
  cooked and
  crumbled
2 hard-cooked eggs,
  chopped
1½ cups grated
  Cheddar cheese
½ cup salted
  peanuts, chopped
3 tablespoons salad
  dressing or
  mayonnaise
1 tablespoon
  half-and-half
Salt and pepper
1 medium head
  lettuce
1 can (10 oz) small
  potatoes, drained
  and sliced
2 ripe tomatoes,
  sliced

Combine the bacon, eggs, cheese,
peanuts, salad dressing and half-and-
half in a bowl and mix well. Season
with salt and pepper to taste.

Arrange the lettuce leaves around
the edge of a serving platter. Pile the
bacon and cheese mixture in the center. Arrange the potato and tomato
slices around the bacon salad. Garnish
with parsley if desired.

4 servings

77

Chick Pea and Cheese Mix

½ lb dried chick peas
½ teaspoon prepared
  mustard
½ teaspoon sugar
1 tablespoon wine
  vinegar
4 tablespoons olive
  oil
Salt and pepper
1 onion, finely
  chopped
2 cloves garlic,
  minced
1 sweet red pepper,
  seeded and sliced
1 green pepper,
  seeded and sliced
2 tablespoons
  chopped mixed
  herbs
⅓ lb havarti,
  Monterey Jack or
  Cheddar cheese,
  cubed

Soak the chick peas in cold water overnight. Drain and place them in a saucepan. Cover with cold water, bring to a boil over high heat and boil for 10 minutes. Reduce the heat, cover and simmer for 1 hour, or until the peas are tender.

Meanwhile, make the dressing. Blend together the mustard and sugar and stir in the vinegar until smooth. Beat in the oil and season with salt and pepper.

Drain the chick peas, then rinse in cold water and transfer to a salad or serving bowl. Add the onion, garlic, peppers, herbs and cheese and stir in until roughly mixed.

Pour the dressing over the salad and toss well. Garnish with chopped parsley if desired.

4 servings

Fruit and Cheese Salad

2 red apples
Juice of 1 lemon
½ honeydew melon
1 can (8 oz) pineapple
   slices, drained and
   chopped
¼ cup dates, pitted
   and chopped
2 tablespoons diced
   cucumber
2 stalks celery,
   chopped
⅓ lb Gouda or other
   firm cheese, cubed
⅔ cup plain yogurt
1 teaspoon sugar
   (optional)

Core and slice the apples; toss in lemon juice to prevent discoloration. Remove the rind and seeds from the melon; dice the flesh or scoop into balls.

In a large mixing bowl, toss the apples in the lemon juice with the melon, pineapple, dates, cucumber, celery and cheese. Stir in the yogurt and sugar and toss well.

Pile the salad into a lettuce-lined serving bowl.
4 servings

Cauliflower and Mushroom Salad

½ lb mushrooms,
  thinly sliced
Juice of 1 lemon
1 small head
  cauliflower, cut
  into flowerets
2 onions, finely
  chopped
Salt and pepper
1 to 2 tablespoons
  olive oil
⅔ cup French
  dressing
  (see page 81)

In a large salad bowl, combine the mushrooms and lemon juice and toss to coat mushrooms. Add the cauliflower and onions; season with salt and pepper and toss.

Blend the olive oil with the French dressing and pour over the vegetables. Let marinate for 30 minutes, tossing occasionally.

If desired, sprinkle with paprika just before serving. This salad is particularly good with fish.

4 servings

French Dressing

1¾ cups olive oil or
    corn oil
6 tablespoons red or
    white wine
    vinegar, or ¼ cup
    wine vinegar and
    2 tablespoons
    lemon juice
¾ teaspoon salt
Freshly ground
    pepper to taste
1½ teaspoons sugar
2 cloves garlic,
    crushed
1 teaspoon Dijon
    mustard

Place all ingredients in a bowl and beat together thoroughly with a wire whisk. Or, place the ingredients in a large screw-top jar and shake vigorously. Always give a final shake or mixing just before serving.

Makes about 2 cups

81

DESSERTS

Family Fruit Salad

2 red apples, sliced
2 bananas, sliced
Grated rind and juice
  of 1 lemon
1 can (8¾ oz) sliced
  peaches
1 can (8¼ oz)
  pineapple chunks
2 oranges, sliced

Toss the apple and banana slices in the lemon juice in a large glass serving dish. Add the peaches and pineapple along with their syrup. Add the oranges with any juice. Toss the fruit and sprinkle with the lemon rind. Chill for at least 1 hour before serving.
6 servings

Baked Banana Splits

4 bananas
Juice of ½ lemon
3 oz semi-sweet
   chocolate,
   coarsely grated
TOPPING:
Whipped cream or
   ice cream
Chopped walnuts

Peel the bananas and split lengthwise without cutting through. Sprinkle with lemon juice. Spoon the grated chocolate into the banana splits. Wrap each banana separately in foil and place on a baking sheet.

Bake in a 350° oven for 20 minutes. Unwrap and serve with whipped cream and chopped walnuts.

4 servings

Baked Bananas with Rum

8 large bananas
1 tablespoon sugar
½ cup white rum
1½ cups heavy
  cream
2 cups crushed
  macaroons
¼ cup chopped
  almonds
2 tablespoons butter,
  melted

Split the bananas in half lengthwise, then cut in half crosswise. Place the bananas in a baking dish and sprinkle them with the sugar and rum. Bake in a 325° oven for 15 minutes.

Pour the cream over the bananas. Combine the macaroons and the almonds and sprinkle over the bananas, then top with the melted butter.

Return to the oven and bake for 20 minutes longer. Serve hot.

6 to 8 servings

Fruit Brûlée

3 tablespoons
   granulated sugar
   (or to taste)
6 tablespoons water
1 tablespoon lemon
   juice
1½ to 2 lb mixed
   seasonal fresh
   fruit, sliced
1½ cups heavy
   cream
¼ cup packed brown
   sugar

In a small saucepan, dissolve the granulated sugar in the water over low heat. Stir in the lemon juice and remove from the heat.

Pile the prepared fruit into a shallow flameproof casserole. Pour the sugar syrup over the fruit and stir. Gently press the fruit down into the casserole and level the top.

Whip the cream until it forms stiff peaks. Spread it over the fruit and chill until just before serving.

To serve, sprinkle the brown sugar over the top of the casserole and place under a broiler until the sugar melts. Serve immediately.

4 to 6 servings

Baked Apples

4 medium tart
   apples, cored
1 teaspoon ground
   cinnamon
2 tablespoons butter
¼ cup powdered
   sugar
1 egg yolk
½ cup ground
   almonds
Grated rind of
   1 orange
3 tablespoons brown
   sugar
4 to 6 tablespoons
   water

Using a sharp knife, make a horizontal cut around the circumference of each apple at its widest point. Stand the apples in an ovenproof dish and sprinkle cinnamon into the cavities.

Cream the butter with the powdered sugar, egg yolk, almonds and orange rind and spoon into the apples. Top with the brown sugar.

Pour the water into the dish and bake in a 350° oven for 45 minutes to 1 hour, or until the apples are tender.

4 servings

Marinated Fruit Compote

15 dried figs,
  chopped
15 dried pitted dates,
  chopped
½ cup blanched
  hazelnuts
½ cup blanched
  almonds
½ cup honey
⅓ cup kirsch or
  brandy
1 large honeydew
  melon, halved and
  seeded

Combine the figs, dates, nuts, honey and kirsch in a large glass serving bowl. Allow to soften for at least 3 hours, stirring occasionally.

Using a melon baller, scoop out the flesh of the honeydew or cut it into cubes. Add to the fruit and stir well. Chill for about 1 hour before serving. Serve with cream if desired.

6 servings

Rhubarb and Strawberry Cobbler

1 lb rhubarb,
  chopped
1 pint strawberries,
  sliced
½ cup sugar
1 teaspoon ground
  cinnamon
3 tablespoons
  shortening
1 cup all-purpose
  flour
1 tablespoon sugar
1½ teaspoons
  baking powder
½ teaspoon salt
½ cup milk

Place the rhubarb and strawberries in a large saucepan with just enough water to cover the bottom of the pan. Add ½ cup sugar and cook over moderate heat for 5 minutes, or until the fruit is tender. Stir in the cinnamon and transfer the fruit to a casserole.

Combine the shortening, flour, 1 tablespoon sugar, baking powder and salt and work together with a fork until the mixture resembles fine crumbs. Stir in the milk.

Drop the dough onto the fruit mixture by 4 spoonfuls. Brush with a little additional milk. Bake in a 400° oven for 15 to 25 minutes, or until the topping is firm and golden brown. Serve hot.

4 servings

Bread Pudding

2 eggs, beaten
2 cups milk
½ cup packed brown
   sugar
1 teaspoon vanilla
1 teaspoon ground
   cinnamon
¼ teaspoon salt
2 cups cubed day-old
   or dry bread
1 cup mixed dried
   fruit

Combine the beaten eggs, milk, brown sugar, vanilla, cinnamon and salt in a large mixing bowl. Stir to combine well.

Add the bread cubes and mix thoroughly. Gently stir in the mixed dried fruit.

Transfer the mixture to a well-greased 2-quart casserole. Bake in a 350° oven for 30 to 40 minutes, until firm to the touch and golden. Serve hot with heavy cream.

6 servings

NOTE: Leftover bread pudding is delicious served cold with whipped cream or softened ice cream. It can also be reheated.

One-Step Layer Cake

½ cup butter,
  softened
1¼ cups sugar
1 teaspoon vanilla
3 eggs
2 cups all-purpose
  flour
1 tablespoon baking
  powder
½ teaspoon salt
1 cup milk
Butter Frosting
  (see Butterfly
  Cupcakes, right)

Combine the butter, sugar, vanilla, eggs, flour, baking powder, salt and milk in a large mixing bowl and beat with an electric beater at high speed for 2 to 3 minutes, or until smooth.

Divide the batter between two greased and floured 8-inch layer pans. Bake in a 350° oven for 30 to 35 minutes, or until a wooden pick inserted in the center of each cake comes out clean. Invert onto a wire rack to cool.

Spread the Butter Frosting on one layer. Top with the second layer and frost the side and top of the cake.

Variations: Add one of the following to the basic ingredients: ¼ cup unsweetened cocoa dissolved in 1 tablespoon hot water; or 2 teaspoons instant coffee dissolved in 1 tablespoon hot water.

Butterfly Cupcakes

Batter for One-Step
  Layer Cake (left)
BUTTER FROSTING:
6 tablespoons butter,
  softened
3 cups powdered
  sugar
1½ to 2 tablespoons
  milk
1 teaspoon flavoring
  (see note)
Powdered sugar for
  sprinkling

Grease eighteen 2½-inch muffin pans or line with paper cups and fill halfway with batter. Bake in a 375° oven for 15 to 18 minutes, or until done. Transfer to a wire rack and let cool.

Meanwhile, prepare the Butter Frosting. Beat the butter, sugar and milk together until very smooth. Stir in the flavoring.

Cut a ½-inch slice off the top of each cupcake and pipe or spoon a little of the frosting on top of each cupcake. Cut the ½-inch slices in half and place at an angle in the frosting to resemble butterfly wings. Sprinkle with powdered sugar.

18 cupcakes

NOTE: Flavor the frosting with any of the following: 1 teaspoon vanilla; 1 teaspoon almond extract; or 1 teaspoon instant coffee powder dissolved in a little hot water.

Chocolate Fudge Pudding

FUDGE TOPPING:
3 tablespoons butter
3 tablespoons soft dark brown sugar
2 tablespoons dark corn syrup
⅓ cup unsweetened cocoa
2 tablespoons half-and-half
½ cup walnuts, finely chopped
CAKE MIXTURE:
2 eggs
½ cup granulated sugar
½ cup butter
1 cup all-purpose flour
2 teaspoons baking powder
½ teaspoon salt

Combine the butter, brown sugar, syrup, cocoa, half-and-half and nuts in a small heavy-bottomed saucepan. Heat gently, stirring constantly, until boiling; boil for 30 seconds. Pour into a greased 8 × 8-inch cake pan or a greased 1½-quart ring mold. Let cool.

Mix the eggs, sugar, butter, flour, baking powder and salt in a large mixing bowl and beat with a wooden spoon for 2 minutes. Pour onto the cooled fudge mixture and spread evenly over it with a spatula.

Bake in a 325° oven for 40 to 45 minutes, or until well risen, golden brown and firm to the touch. Leave in the pan for 5 minutes.

Invert onto a serving plate. The fudge becomes a soft topping that runs down the sides of the cake. Serve hot, with cream if desired.

6 to 8 servings

Moist Chocolate Layer Cake

1 cup butter
2 cups granulated sugar
2 teaspoons vanilla
4 oz unsweetened chocolate
5 eggs
2¼ cups cake flour, sifted
1 teaspoon baking soda
1 teaspoon salt
1 cup buttermilk
CHOCOLATE
BUTTER FROSTING:
1⅔ cups powdered sugar, sifted
2 tablespoons cocoa mixed with 2 tablespoons boiling water
½ cup butter, softened
1 tablespoon milk (if needed)

Cream the butter and granulated sugar in a mixer bowl until light and fluffy. Blend in the vanilla. Melt the chocolate in the top of a double boiler; cool. Blend chocolate into the butter mixture. Add the eggs, one at a time, beating well after each addition.

Sift together the flour, soda and salt. Gradually stir into the creamed mixture, a little at a time, alternating with the buttermilk and beating well after each addition.

Pour into two greased and lightly floured 9-inch round layer pans. Bake in a 350° oven for 25 to 40 minutes. Turn out onto a rack to cool.

To prepare the frosting, mix the sugar, cocoa and butter. If necessary beat in the milk until of the desired consistency. Spread the frosting between the two layers and use the remainder to frost the top and side of the cake.

INDEX